RANJOT SINGH CHAHAL

# The Ultimate Guide on How to Become Famous and Make Your Mark

# Contents

# Chapter 1: Defining Fame: Understanding the Different Paths to Recognition

Fame has always been an elusive concept, yet it holds immense significance in modern society. The allure of recognition, admiration, and influence has driven individuals to seek fame throughout history. However, fame is a multifaceted phenomenon that manifests in various forms and through diverse paths. In this chapter, we will delve into the nature of fame, explore its different types, and provide guidance on identifying one's passion – a crucial step towards achieving recognition.

Section 1: The Nature of Fame

To comprehend fame fully, we must examine its meaning and significance in contemporary society. Fame embodies more than just the state of being widely known or celebrated; it encompasses the sway and impact an individual holds over others. It goes beyond mere visibility and delves into the realm of influence, affording individuals the power to shape opinions, ideologies, and trends on a grand scale.

Furthermore, fame often comes with both benefits and drawbacks. On the positive side, it provides financial opportunities, social validation, and the ability to effect change. However, it also brings increased scrutiny, loss of privacy, and the potential for exploitation. Understanding this dichotomy is essential for aspiring individuals on their quest for recognition.

Section 2: Types of Fame

Fame manifests through different avenues, each with its own unique characteristics and paths to success. Exploring these types can help individuals identify the fields where they can make a name for themselves. Here are some of the most notable avenues to achieve fame:

1. Entertainment: The world of entertainment, encompassing film, music, television, and theater, has long been a fertile ground for fame. Through performance, storytelling, and artistic expression, entertainers captivate audiences and carve out their place in the limelight. Acting icons like Meryl Streep and Leonardo DiCaprio, music legends like Beyoncé and Michael Jackson, and acclaimed directors like Steven Spielberg symbolize the heights of fame in the entertainment industry.

2. Sports: Athletes possess exceptional physical prowess, and through their dedication, skill, and unwavering determination, they elevate themselves to the status of sporting legends. From football star Cristiano Ronaldo to basketball phenom LeBron James to tennis icon Serena Williams, these athletes transcend

the realm of sports and become global symbols of achievement and fame.

3. Social Media: With the rise of the digital age, social media has become a prominent platform for achieving fame. Internet influencers, YouTube stars, and Instagram celebrities have amassed large followings by creating compelling content and engaging with their audiences. Examples include beauty guru James Charles, vlogger PewDiePie, and lifestyle influencer Chiara Ferragni.

4. Activism and Philanthropy: Making a difference in the world can also lead to fame. Activists and philanthropists who fight for social justice, advocate for marginalized communities, or dedicate themselves to humanitarian causes often gain recognition for their efforts. Nobel Peace Prize laureate Malala Yousafzai, environmental activist Greta Thunberg, and philanthropist Bill Gates exemplify fame through their impactful work.

5. Science and Innovation: Pioneering breakthroughs and advancements in science and innovation can also propel individuals to fame. Notable figures such as Albert Einstein, Steve Jobs, and Elon Musk gained recognition for their revolutionary ideas and contributions to their respective fields.

Section 3: Identifying Your Passion

Finding the field where one wants to make a name for themselves is essential on the journey to fame. Identifying your passion allows you to channel your efforts and talents towards a meaningful pursuit, increasing the likelihood of success and fulfillment. Here are some steps to help in this endeavor:

1. Self-Reflection: Take time to introspect and understand your interests, values, and strengths. Consider what activities or subjects bring you joy, where you excel, and what you are willing to invest significant time and effort in. Reflecting on these aspects will help unveil potential passions.

2. Experimentation: Actively explore various fields and opportunities to gain firsthand experience. This may involve taking up hobbies, attending workshops, or volunteering in different domains. Experimentation helps you discover what resonates with you and allows you to make an informed decision regarding your passion.

3. Research and Exposure: Conduct extensive research on the fields that intrigue you the most. Immerse yourself in books, documentaries, articles, and interviews to gain deeper insights into different industries. This exposure helps you understand the requirements, challenges, and potential opportunities within each field.

4. Seeking Mentors and Role Models: Interacting with mentors and seeking guidance from individuals who have achieved success in your desired field can provide valuable insights. Mentors can offer advice, share their experiences, and provide clarity on the path towards recognition.

5. Taking Action: Once you have identified your passion, it is vital to take consistent and deliberate action towards your goals. Set achievable milestones, develop a plan, and remain dedicated

to your chosen path. Remember, perseverance and continuous learning are essential for achieving recognition.

Conclusion:

In this chapter, we have explored the nature of fame, the different types of fame, and the process of identifying one's passion. Fame is a complex and multifaceted phenomenon, and understanding its nuances is crucial for those who aspire to achieve recognition. By recognizing the significance of fame and exploring various avenues, individuals can choose their path wisely and pursue their passions with purpose. The next chapter will delve into the essential qualities and skills required to thrive on the path to fame.

# Chapter 2: Building Your Brand: Crafting a Memorable and Marketable Identity

In today's highly competitive world, building a strong brand is essential for standing out from the crowd and achieving success in your chosen field. This chapter focuses on the key aspects of building your brand, including identifying your unique selling point, personal branding, and presenting yourself in an authentic and appealing way.

1. Identifying Your Unique Selling Point:

To build a successful brand, it is crucial to identify and emphasize your unique selling point (USP). Your USP is what sets you apart from others in your chosen field and makes you memorable to your audience. It could be a particular skill, experience, or approach that distinguishes you from your competitors.

For example, let's say you are a freelance graphic designer. Your USP could be your ability to seamlessly blend traditional and digital art techniques, offering clients a distinctive and innovative design style that sets you apart from other designers.

Identifying your USP requires self-reflection, market analysis, and understanding your target audience. By understanding what makes you unique and aligning it with market demands, you can effectively differentiate yourself and create a compelling brand identity.

2. Personal Branding:

Personal branding involves developing a persona that effectively represents your skills, values, and overall image. It is about creating a consistent and authentic brand that resonates with your target audience, making you more memorable and marketable.

To begin developing your personal brand, it is important to define your values, strengths, and passions. Consider the following questions:

- What are your core values? What do you want to be known for?
  - What are your strengths and expertise in your field?
  - What excites you and brings you joy in your work?

By answering these questions, you can shape your personal brand persona in a way that is genuine and aligned with your values. This will enable you to attract the right audience and build long-lasting connections.

Building a strong online presence is an integral part of personal branding. Social media platforms, professional networks like LinkedIn, and personal websites are valuable tools for showcasing your work, sharing your expertise, and engaging with your audience.

3. Image and Style:

Your image and style play a crucial role in building your brand. How you present yourself visually and verbally can leave a lasting impression on your audience. It is important to strike a balance between authenticity and visual appeal, ensuring that your brand resonates with your target audience.

When developing your brand's image and style, consider the following elements:

- Logo and Visual Identity: Your logo is the visual representation of your brand and should be carefully designed to reflect your brand's personality and values. Choose colors, fonts, and imagery that align with your brand's identity and create a consistent visual language across all your marketing materials.

- Tone of Voice: Your brand's tone of voice reflects your personality and sets the tone for your communication. Whether it's casual and friendly or professional and authoritative, ensure that your tone remains consistent across different channels to build a recognizable brand voice.

- Website and Collateral: Your website acts as the central hub for your brand and should reflect your image and style. It should be visually appealing, user-friendly, and provide a seamless experience for visitors. Additionally, any printed materials, such as business cards or brochures, should be designed in a way that is consistent with your brand's visual identity.

For instance, consider a fashion brand targeting a young and trendy audience. Their logo would likely be modern, edgy, and use vibrant colors. The tone of voice would be casual and relatable, reflecting the brand's youthful image and building a connection with the target audience.

4. Consistency and Cohesion:

Consistency is a critical aspect of building a memorable brand. It refers to presenting a unified and cohesive image across all platforms and touchpoints. Consistency helps build trust, reliability, and recognition among your target audience.

To achieve consistency, it is crucial to establish brand guidelines that outline the preferred colors, fonts, imagery, and overall visual style of your brand. These guidelines act as a reference point for all marketing materials, ensuring that your brand's identity remains consistent across various channels.

For example, if you have chosen a bold and vibrant color palette for your brand, it should be consistently applied in your logo, website, social media posts, and any other marketing materials. This cohesion creates a strong visual identity that is easily recognizable and associated with your brand.

5. Leveraging Storytelling:

Storytelling is a powerful tool for building a memorable brand. By crafting a compelling narrative around your brand, you can connect with your audience on an emotional level and leave a lasting impact.

Consider the story behind your brand. What motivated you to pursue your chosen field? Do you have a unique journey or experience that has shaped your skills and values? Sharing these stories creates relatability and helps establish a deeper connection with your audience.

Storytelling can be incorporated across various brand touch-points, such as your website's About page, social media posts, blog articles, and even in conversations with clients. By weaving your brand's story into your messaging, you create a sense of authenticity, credibility, and differentiation.

6. Establishing Thought Leadership:

Building a memorable brand also involves positioning yourself as a thought leader in your industry or niche. Thought leadership is about offering valuable insights, expertise, and perspectives that establish you as an authority and go-to resource for your target audience.

To establish thought leadership, consider the following strategies:

- Consistently sharing informative and helpful content through blog articles, videos, podcasts, or social media posts.
    - Participating in industry events, conferences, or webinars as a speaker or panelist.
    - Engaging in conversations and sharing insights on relevant online platforms and communities.
    - Collaborating with other experts or brands in your field to showcase your expertise.

By consistently providing valuable information and insights, you position yourself as a trusted expert, reinforcing your brand's credibility and memorability.

Conclusion:

Building a memorable and marketable brand requires a strategic approach that encompasses various elements. From identifying your unique selling point to developing your personal brand, and presenting yourself in an authentic and appealing way, each aspect contributes to the overall success of your brand.

Remember, building a brand is a continuous process that evolves over time. Stay true to your values, adapt to market demands, and consistently communicate your brand's identity across all touchpoints. By crafting a memorable and marketable brand, you increase your chances of standing out, attracting your target audience, and achieving long-term success in your chosen field.

# Chapter 3: Navigating the Industry: Strategies for Success

In the competitive landscape of any industry, it is crucial to have a deep understanding of the trends, key players, and dynamics that drive success. This chapter explores the importance of researching your industry, establishing valuable connections through networking and collaboration, and leveraging various platforms for self-promotion. These strategies are crucial for navigating the industry and positioning yourself for success.

Section 1: Researching Your Industry

Understanding and staying up-to-date with the latest trends and developments in your industry is essential for strategic decision-making and maintaining a competitive edge. Here are some key steps to effectively research your industry:

1. Identify key industry trends: Monitor industry-specific publications, news outlets, market reports, and social media platforms to identify emerging trends. Pay attention to new technologies, consumer preferences, market dynamics, and regulatory changes.

Example:  In the fashion industry, researching trends can involve analyzing runway shows, examining street styles, and following influencers and fashion bloggers on social media to stay current with the latest fashion trends.

2. Study your competitors: Analyze your competitors' strategies, products, and marketing techniques. Identify their strengths and weaknesses to gain insights into industry best practices and potential areas for differentiation.

Example: If you are starting a new restaurant, researching your competitors involves evaluating their menus, prices, customer service, ambiance, and marketing efforts to develop a unique value proposition.

3. Identify key players: Identify and study the leading companies and individuals in your industry.  Understand their market position, business models, success factors, and strategies. This knowledge can help you identify potential mentors, partners, or career opportunities.

Example:  In the technology industry, understanding the key players would involve studying companies like Apple, Google, Microsoft, and their respective product lines, acquisitions, innovations, and market share.

Section 2: Networking and Collaboration

Establishing valuable connections and partnerships is a crucial aspect of achieving success in any industry. Networking allows you to tap into opportunities, gain support, and expand your reach. Here are some strategies for effective networking and collaboration:

1. Attend industry events: Participate in conferences, trade shows, seminars, and workshops relevant to your industry. These events provide opportunities to meet industry experts, potential clients, partners, and investors.

Example: A software developer attending a technology conference can network with fellow developers, industry leaders, recruiters, and venture capitalists, thereby fostering collaborations and identifying potential job opportunities.

2. Join professional organizations: Become a member of industry-specific professional associations or organizations. These platforms offer networking events, workshops, and mentorship programs that facilitate connections and offer valuable resources.

Example: A marketing professional joining a marketing association can benefit from networking events, industry insights, and mentorship opportunities, allowing them to build relationships with key players and stay updated on the latest marketing practices.

3. Utilize online platforms: Leverage online networking platforms, such as LinkedIn, to connect with professionals in your industry. Join relevant groups, contribute to discussions, and showcase your expertise to expand your network and attract potential collaborations.

Example: A freelance graphic designer can utilize LinkedIn groups dedicated to design and creative industries to connect with potential clients, collaborators, and mentors.

Section 3: Self-Promotion

In today's digital age, self-promotion through various platforms is essential for gaining exposure and showcasing your talent. Here are some key strategies for effective self-promotion:

1. Build an online presence: Create a professional website, blog, or portfolio to showcase your work, expertise, and accomplishments. This online presence acts as a virtual resume and enables potential clients, employers, or collaborators to learn more about you.

Example: A photographer can create a website featuring their best photographs, client testimonials, and a blog sharing their photography techniques and experiences, attracting potential clients and collaborators.

2. Engage on social media: Utilize social media platforms, such as Instagram, Twitter, or YouTube, to share your work, thoughts, and interact with your audience. Use relevant hashtags, engage with industry influencers, and participate in industry-related discussions to increase your visibility and build a following.

Example: A fitness coach can use Instagram to post workout videos, share fitness tips, and engage with followers through comments and direct messages, establishing themselves as an authority in the fitness industry.

3. Collaborate with others: Collaborating with other professionals or influencers in your industry can help expand your reach and attract new opportunities. By partnering on projects, you can tap into their audience and gain exposure to a wider market.

Example: A makeup artist can collaborate with a popular beauty influencer to create a makeup tutorial video. This collaboration not only showcases their skills but also exposes them to the influencer's audience, potentially leading to new clients or brand partnerships.

4. Seek media coverage: Actively pursue media coverage through press releases, contacting journalists, or pitching story ideas. Getting featured in industry publications or media outlets can significantly enhance your visibility and credibility.

Example: An entrepreneur launching a new tech startup can reach out to tech publications or journalists to generate press coverage and raise awareness about their innovative product or service.

5. Build and nurture relationships: As you promote yourself, prioritize building genuine and meaningful relationships with your audience, clients, and industry peers. Engage with your followers, attend industry events, and offer support and assistance when needed. These relationships can lead to referrals and long-term collaborations.

Example: A graphic designer who consistently provides high-quality work, responds promptly to client inquiries, and maintains positive relationships is more likely to receive word-of-mouth recommendations and repeat business.

By combining thorough industry research, effective networking, and strategic self-promotion, you can position yourself for success and stand out in your chosen industry. Remember that establishing a strong reputation and continuously honing your skills are also critical elements for long-term success.

# Chapter 4: Mastering Your Craft: Hone Your Skills

In today's rapidly evolving world, mastering your craft and honing your skills is crucial for success. Regardless of the field, continuous learning and improvement, seeking professional guidance, and overcoming challenges are vital aspects of skill development. In this chapter, we will delve into these three key areas, exploring their importance and providing practical examples to help you grasp their significance.

Continuous Learning and Improvement:

1. The Importance of Practice:
   One of the fundamental ways to hone your skills is through practice. Continuous practice allows you to refine your technique, build muscle memory, and improve proficiency. Whether you are a musician, athlete, or artist, deliberate practice is the key to mastery.

Example 1: Musician
   A budding musician wants to become a skilled pianist. To achieve this, they commit to practicing for two hours a day,

focusing on various techniques, scales, and pieces. With each day of practice, they notice gradual improvements in their accuracy, speed, and musicality. Over time, they build a solid foundation and become a proficient pianist.

Example 2: Athlete

An aspiring athlete aims to improve their basketball skills. They dedicate themselves to daily practice routines, working on shooting, dribbling, and agility exercises. As they consistently practice, their shooting percentage increases, their ball handling becomes more precise, and their overall performance on the court improves.

2. Staying Updated:

Skills and knowledge are not static. It's essential to stay updated with the latest developments in your field to remain relevant and competitive. Continuous learning allows you to adapt to changing trends, technologies, and best practices.

Example 1: Software Developer

A software developer actively participates in industry forums, attends conferences, and explores online resources to stay up-to-date with the latest programming languages and frameworks. By continuously learning new technologies, they enhance their skills and are able to create innovative solutions for their clients.

Example 2: Marketing Professional

A marketing professional subscribes to industry newsletters, regularly reads books on marketing strategies, and engages in networking events to keep themselves informed about emerging trends. By continuously learning and staying updated, they can develop effective marketing campaigns that resonate with the target audience.

Training and Education:

1. Seeking Professional Guidance:
   While self-directed learning is valuable, seeking professional guidance can accelerate your skill development. Enlisting the help of mentors, coaches, and trainers provides structured guidance, expert advice, and personalized feedback.

Example 1: Entrepreneur
   An aspiring entrepreneur seeks the guidance of a seasoned business mentor who has successfully launched multiple ventures. The mentor provides insights, guides them through business planning, and shares valuable lessons based on their own experiences. With the mentor's guidance, the entrepreneur avoids common pitfalls and makes better-informed decisions, thus enhancing their chances of success.

Example 2: Professional Speaker
   A novice public speaker enrolls in a training program conducted by an experienced speaker. The program covers various aspects of public speaking, including voice modulation, body language, and storytelling techniques. Through the guidance and feedback of the trainer, the novice speaker gains confidence, refines their delivery style, and becomes a compelling public speaker.

2. Formal Education:
   Formal education, such as degrees, certifications, and work-

shops, can provide foundational knowledge and specialized skills, giving you a competitive edge in your field.

Example 1: Healthcare Professional

A nurse pursues a master's degree in nursing administration to gain advanced skills in leadership, healthcare management, and policy implementation. With this formal education, they are prepared to take on leadership roles in hospitals or healthcare organizations.

Example 2: Graphic Designer

A graphic designer enrolls in a specialized workshop that focuses on the latest design software and techniques. By learning from industry experts, they acquire new design skills, keep up with design trends, and expand their professional portfolio.

Overcoming Challenges:

1. Adopting a Resilient Mindset:

Challenges and setbacks are inevitable on the journey to skill mastery. Adopting a resilient mindset allows you to bounce back from failures, persevere through obstacles, and learn from mistakes.

Example 1: Entrepreneurial Failure

An entrepreneur faced several failures in their entrepreneurial journey, including the collapse of a previous business. Instead of giving up, they embrace the failures as valuable learning experiences. They analyze their mistakes, adapt their strategies, and launch a new business that eventually becomes a success.

Example 2: Athlete's Injury

An athlete suffers a significant injury that sidelines them for months. Instead of getting discouraged, they focus on their rehabilitation, work closely with physiotherapists, and mentally prepare themselves for a successful comeback. Through their resilience and determination, they return to their sport, stronger and more skilled than before.

2. Seeking Support:

Overcoming challenges becomes more accessible when you seek support from peers, mentors, and your professional network. They can provide advice, offer encouragement, and share their own experiences, which can inspire you to persevere.

Example 1: Creative Writer

A writer faces writer's block and feels demotivated to continue their work. They seek support from fellow writers, joining a writing group where they can discuss their struggles and share ideas. Collaborating with other writers helps reignite their passion for writing, provides them with constructive feedback, and helps them overcome their creative hurdles.

Example 2: IT Professional

An IT professional encounters a complex technical problem that they cannot solve independently. They reach out to their network of colleagues and fellow professionals, seeking input and advice. Through collaboration and brainstorming, they find a solution that resolves the issue.

3.Continuous Improvement Through Feedback:

Receiving constructive feedback is a crucial aspect of skill development. Whether from mentors, colleagues, or peers, feedback provides valuable insights that can guide your improvement journey.

Example 1: Graphic Designer A graphic designer regularly shares their work with a mentor and colleagues, seeking feedback on their designs. Constructive criticism helps them identify areas for improvement, refine their design choices, and stay updated with industry standards. This continuous feedback loop contributes to their ongoing growth and excellence in graphic design.

Example 2: Project Manager A project manager actively encourages team members to provide feedback on project processes and collaboration. By listening to the team's input, the project manager identifies areas where adjustments can be made, streamlines workflows, and enhances overall project efficiency. This commitment to continuous improvement through feedback ensures the team's success and fosters a culture of collaboration.

In conclusion, mastering your craft involves a dynamic process of continuous learning, seeking professional guidance, and overcoming challenges. By embracing these three key areas, you pave the way for sustained growth, excellence, and success in your chosen field. Remember, the journey to mastery is ongoing, and each step forward contributes to your evolution as a skilled and accomplished professional.

# Chapter 5: Captivating Your Audience: Winning Hearts and Minds

In today's highly competitive world, captivating your audience has become an essential skill for anyone looking to make an impact. Whether you are a public speaker, a content creator, or a social media influencer, the ability to connect with your audience on an emotional level is crucial for winning their hearts and minds. This chapter will delve deeper into the techniques and strategies that can help you develop your personal story, create engaging content, and build effective relationships with your followers.

1. Developing Your Personal Story:

One of the most powerful ways to connect with your audience is through storytelling. Your personal story allows you to share your experiences, values, and motivations, creating a strong emotional connection with your audience. Here are a few ways to develop your personal story:

a) Authenticity: Your story should be genuine and authentic. People can easily spot inauthenticity and it can damage your credibility. Be honest and open about your journey, including both your successes and failures.

Example: Sarah, a successful entrepreneur, shares her story of overcoming adversity and the challenges she faced while building her business. By being transparent about her experiences, she creates a relatable and inspiring narrative that resonates with her audience.

b) Emotionally Engaging: To captivate your audience, your personal story should evoke emotions. Share moments of triumph, vulnerability, and self-discovery that make your audience feel connected to you.

Example: John, a motivational speaker, shares his personal struggles with mental health. By discussing his own battles and the steps he took to overcome them, he elicits empathy and support from his audience.

c) Relevance: Tailor your story to your audience's interests and needs. By understanding their aspirations and challenges, you can make your story more relatable and impactful, ensuring it resonates with them on a deeper level.

Example: Jenny, a fitness influencer, shares her personal journey of losing weight and transforming her lifestyle. She focuses on the physical and mental benefits of exercise and creates content that addresses the specific concerns her audience may have, such as time constraints and self-doubt.

2. Engaging Content Creation:

Creating captivating and relatable content is essential to keeping your audience engaged and interested. Here are some strategies to help you create engaging content:

a) Know Your Audience: Understanding your audience's demographics, interests, and preferences is crucial for tailoring your content to their needs. Conduct surveys, analyze data, and engage directly with your audience to gather insights.

Example: A cooking blogger surveys their followers to understand their dietary restrictions and preferences. Armed with this knowledge, they create recipes that cater to their audience's needs, ensuring their content remains relevant and engaging.

b) Tell Compelling Stories: Incorporate storytelling into your content creation process. Use narratives, case studies, and personal anecdotes to make your content more relatable and captivating.

Example: A travel vlogger shares their experiences through a series of stories, ranging from exhilarating adventures to cultural encounters. By weaving narratives into their content, they transport their audience to different destinations, sparking their curiosity and desire to explore.

c) Visual Appeal: Make sure your content is visually appealing. Use high-quality images, videos, and graphics that complement your message and capture your audience's attention.

Example: A fashion influencer collaborates with professional photographers to create visually stunning and aesthetically pleasing photoshoots. By showcasing eye-catching visuals, they not only captivate their audience but also inspire them with new fashion ideas.

3. Communication Skills:

Building effective relationships and engaging with your followers is essential for captivating your audience. Here are some communication skills to help you in this regard:

a) Active Listening: Engage in active listening by paying attention to your audience's needs, concerns, and feedback. Show empathy and respond genuinely to their inquiries and comments.

Example: A customer service representative actively listens to customer complaints, demonstrating empathy, and offering effective solutions. Their ability to address concerns and provide helpful insights builds strong customer relationships.

b) Two-Way Communication: Encourage dialogue with your audience. Respond to comments, messages, and emails promptly and cater to their needs. Make them feel heard and valued.

Example: A YouTuber actively engages with their subscribers through comments and community posts. They encourage discussion and respond personally to try and fulfill their viewers' requests and recommendations.

c) Collaboration and Partnerships: Collaborate with other influencers, brands, or experts in your field. This not only exposes you to new audiences but also enhances your credibility and provides fresh perspectives.

Example:  A beauty blogger collaborates with a well-known skincare brand to create educational content about skincare routines. This collaboration helps build trust with the audience while providing valuable insights from a reputable brand.

4. Emotional Appeal:

To captivate your audience and win their hearts and minds, it is crucial to appeal to their emotions. Emotions have a profound impact on how people perceive and connect with content. Here are some strategies to incorporate emotional appeal into your communication:

a) Storytelling Techniques: Use storytelling techniques to evoke emotions in your audience.  Create narratives that touch on universal themes such as love, hope, fear, or perseverance. Narratives that resonate on an emotional level are more likely to captivate and inspire your audience.

Example: A nonprofit organization shares stories of individuals who have benefited from their work. By highlighting personal struggles and triumphs, they evoke empathy and compassion, compelling people to support their cause.

b) Personalization: Tailor your content to the individual experiences and aspirations of your audience. Understand their pain points, desires, and dreams, and address them in a way that resonates emotionally.

Example: A career coach creates content that addresses the fears and uncertainties of job seekers. By providing guidance, motivation, and personal anecdotes, they create an emotional connection, inspiring people to take action in their own career journeys.

c) Use Visuals Wisely: Visual elements, such as images, videos, and infographics, can enhance the emotional impact of your content. Choose visuals that elicit the desired emotions and reinforce your message effectively.

Example: An animal welfare organization shares heartwarming photos and videos of rescued animals finding their forever homes. These visuals evoke feelings of joy, compassion, and the desire to contribute to the cause.

5. Call-to-Action (CTA):

Effective communication involves guiding your audience towards a specific action. A well-crafted call-to-action prompts your audience to take the desired steps, whether it's to purchase a product, donate to a cause, subscribe to a channel, or share your content. Here are some strategies to create compelling CTAs:

a) Clear and Concise: Make your call-to-action clear and concise. Avoid ambiguity and provide specific instructions to your audience on what you want them to do.

Example: A podcast host concludes each episode by inviting listeners to subscribe, rate, and review the podcast on their preferred platform, ensuring a straightforward and actionable CTA.

b) Sense of Urgency: Instill a sense of urgency in your call-to-action to prompt immediate action. Limited-time offers or deadlines create a need to act swiftly, increasing the likelihood of engagement.

Example: A clothing brand offers a discount code valid for 24 hours only. By emphasizing the time sensitivity of the offer, they motivate their audience to make a purchase without delay.

c) Incentives and Benefits: Highlight the benefits and incentives that your audience will gain by taking the desired action. Whether it's discounts, exclusive content, or access to a community, clearly communicate the value they will receive.

Example: A fitness trainer encourages their followers to join their online fitness program by emphasizing the health benefits, a supportive community, and personalized coaching that participants will gain.

Conclusion:

Winning the hearts and minds of your audience requires a multifaceted approach that involves developing your personal story, creating engaging content, sharpening your communication skills, and leveraging emotional appeal. By connecting with your audience on an emotional level through authentic storytelling, delivering captivating and relatable content, and building effective relationships, you can create a loyal following that is eager to listen, engage, and support your endeavors. Remember, the key is to understand your audience, evoke emotions, provide value, and guide them towards action through compelling and well-crafted CTAs.

# Chapter 6: Managing Fame: Embracing the Responsibilities and Pitfalls

In the modern era, achieving fame has become more accessible than ever before. With the rise of social media platforms and the internet, individuals can quickly gain widespread recognition and exposure. While fame can bring numerous advantages, it also comes with a set of responsibilities and pitfalls. This chapter will delve into the intricacies of managing fame, focusing on maintaining a positive public image and reputation, navigating criticism and hate, and striking a balance between privacy and exposure.

Section 1: Public Image and Reputation

Maintaining a positive and credible persona is crucial for individuals in the public eye. Your public image reflects how others perceive you, and it often shapes their opinions and attitudes towards you. Here are a few strategies for effectively managing your public image:

1. Authenticity: Being true to yourself is essential for building a credible public image. People appreciate individuals who are

genuine and transparent. For example, renowned actor Tom Hanks has consistently been perceived as authentic due to his down-to-earth personality, humility, and sincere approach to his craft.

2. Consistency: Maintaining a consistent image helps establish trust and reliability. It is important to align your actions, statements, and values to avoid confusion or controversy. For instance, Oprah Winfrey has built a reliable public image by consistently promoting empathy, self-improvement, and philanthropy.

3. Intentional Communication: How you communicate with the public plays a significant role in shaping your image. Thoughtful and well-crafted messages can have a positive impact, while careless or offensive remarks can harm your reputation. Effective communication includes engaging with your audience, addressing concerns, and promoting positive values.

4. Branding: Just like businesses, individuals can benefit from building a personal brand. Developing a clear and distinctive identity helps differentiate yourself from others in the same field. Oprah Winfrey's personal brand, for example, centers around empowerment, positivity, and personal growth.

Section 2: Dealing with Criticism and Hate

In the digital age, it is almost inevitable for public figures to face criticism and hate. Online trolls and negative comments can be challenging to navigate, but there are strategies to cope with them effectively:

1. Emotional Resilience: Developing emotional resilience is essential when dealing with criticism. It is vital to remind yourself that not all feedback is genuinely constructive, and some individuals may intentionally try to bring you down. Focus on the opinions of those who genuinely care about your well-being and growth.

2. Selective Engagement: Not every negative comment requires a response. Engaging with trolls often leads to further escalation and wastes valuable energy. Instead, focus on addressing legitimate concerns and maintaining open conversations, fostering a healthier online environment.

3. Constructive Feedback: Differentiating between hateful comments and constructive criticism is crucial. Constructive feedback can offer valuable insights and opportunities for personal and professional growth. Recognize when critique stems from genuine concern and consider incorporating it into your self-improvement journey.

4. Support Network: Surrounding yourself with a positive support network can help you navigate challenging situations. Trusted friends, family, and colleagues can provide emotional support, advice, and perspective to help you deal with criticism more effectively.

Section 3: Balancing Privacy and Exposure

One of the significant challenges of fame is finding a balance between personal privacy and public exposure. Here are some strategies to protect your personal life while still maintaining a public presence:

1. Establishing Boundaries: Clearly defining your boundaries and communicating them to the public is essential. Determine what aspects of your personal life you are comfortable sharing and which are off-limits. By setting clear boundaries, you can ensure that your private life remains protected.

2. Social Media Management: Effectively managing your social media accounts can help strike a balance between privacy and exposure. Consider having separate personal and public accounts or controlling the level of information you share publicly. Emma Watson, for example, keeps her personal social media accounts private and uses public platforms mainly for professional updates.

3. Media Relations: Developing a rapport with the media can help shape the narrative surrounding your personal life. Engage with journalists and reporters who respect your boundaries and values, as they can contribute to maintaining a positive public image while respecting your privacy.

4. Self-Care and Time Off: Taking regular breaks from the public eye is essential for protecting your mental and emotional well-being. Investing in self-care activities, such as hobbies, spending time with loved ones, and pursuing personal interests, can help you maintain a healthy work-life balance.

Conclusion:

Managing fame requires individuals to embrace the responsibilities and pitfalls that come with it. By focusing on maintaining a positive public image, navigating criticism and hate effectively, and striking a balance between privacy and exposure, public figures can adapt to the challenges of fame and lead fulfilling lives both professionally and personally.

# Chapter 7: Longevity and Sustainability: Sustaining Your Fame

In the world of fame and recognition, sustaining one's success over a long period is a challenging task. Many individuals rise to the pinnacle of fame only to fade away into obscurity shortly thereafter. However, in this chapter, we will delve into the strategies and actions necessary for ensuring longevity and sustainability in the realm of fame. We will explore concepts such as diversifying pursuits, reinvention, giving back, and leaving a lasting legacy. Through concrete examples and in-depth analysis, we will provide insights on how you can navigate the unpredictable path of fame and create a lasting impact.

Section 1: Diversifying Your Pursuits

Expanding your influence into different areas can be a key strategy for sustaining your fame. By diversifying your pursuits, you not only broaden your reach but also create multiple streams of income and opportunities for growth. Let's explore this concept further.

Example 1: Beyoncé Knowles

Beyoncé is a remarkable example of diversifying pursuits.

While she initially rose to fame as a singer and member of Destiny's Child, she expanded her influence by venturing into acting, fashion, entrepreneurship, and even social activism. By diversifying her pursuits, Beyoncé has been able to maintain her relevance and sustain her fame over the years.

Example 2: Will Smith

Will Smith is another notable example of diversifying pursuits. He started his career as a rapper and then transitioned into acting, starring in successful films like "Men in Black" and "The Pursuit of Happyness." Smith further diversified by producing films, investing in businesses, and engaging in philanthropic endeavors. His ability to diversify his pursuits has contributed to his sustained fame and success.

Section 2: Reinventing Yourself

Staying relevant and adapting to changing trends is crucial for sustaining your fame. Reinventing yourself allows you to connect with evolving audiences and maintain a fresh image. Let's dive deeper into this concept.

Example 1: Madonna

Madonna has continuously reinvented herself throughout her career, adapting to changing musical trends and cultural shifts. From her early days as a pop icon in the 1980s to exploring different genres like electronica, dance, and even Latin music, Madonna has consistently been at the forefront of reinvention. By reinventing herself, she has sustained her fame and remained relevant over decades.

Example 2: Jay-Z

Jay-Z is an excellent example of reinvention in the music industry. From his early days as a rapper to becoming a successful entrepreneur and music executive, Jay-Z has continually evolved and adapted to the changing landscape of the music industry. By staying innovative and fresh, he has maintained his fame and longevity in an industry known for its fast-paced trends.

## Section 3: Giving Back

Using your fame for positive impact and social change can not only create a meaningful legacy but also help sustain your fame over time. By giving back, you engage with your audience on a deeper level and make a genuine difference in the world. Let's explore this concept further.

## Example 1: Oprah Winfrey

Oprah Winfrey is widely recognized for her philanthropic efforts and using her fame as a force for good. Through the establishment of the Oprah Winfrey Foundation and various charitable initiatives, she has made significant contributions to education, healthcare, and empowerment. By giving back, Oprah has not only created a lasting legacy but also earned the respect and admiration of her audience.

## Example 2: Leonardo DiCaprio

Leonardo DiCaprio has leveraged his fame to advocate for environmental causes and raise awareness about critical issues. Through the creation of the Leonardo DiCaprio Foundation, he has supported numerous conservation projects, climate change initiatives, and biodiversity preservation. DiCaprio's commitment to giving back has not only sustained his fame but also positioned him as a respected environmental activist.

Section 4: Leaving a Lasting Legacy

Creating a lasting legacy is the epitome of sustaining your fame. It entails making a significant impact on society and ensuring that your name and contributions endure beyond your lifetime. Let's explore this concept in more detail.

Example 1: Mahatma Gandhi

Mahatma Gandhi is a timeless example of leaving a lasting legacy. His philosophy of non-violence and civil disobedience continues to inspire generations and has had a profound impact on human rights movements worldwide. Gandhi's legacy of peace and justice has transcended time and solidified his place as one of history's most influential figures.

Example 2: Steve Jobs

Steve Jobs, the co-founder of Apple Inc., revolutionized the world of technology and left an indelible mark on society. His innovative products, such as the iPhone and MacBook, have transformed the way we communicate and interact with technology. By leaving a lasting legacy, Jobs has ensured that his name remains synonymous with groundbreaking innovation and design excellence.

Conclusion:

Sustaining fame requires strategic thinking, adaptability, and a genuine desire to make a positive impact. By diversifying pursuits, reinventing oneself, giving back, and leaving a lasting legacy, individuals can navigate the challenging path of sustained success and create a lasting impact. Through the examples provided in this chapter, we have seen the power of these strategies and how they contribute to the longevity and sustainability of fame. So, whether you're a star, entrepreneur, or public figure, remember the importance of these principles as you carve your path towards sustained fame and achievement.

# Chapter 8: Managing Finances: Building Wealth and Financial Security

Managing finances and building wealth are critical components of achieving financial security. In this chapter, we will delve deep into the various aspects of financial planning, tax and legal considerations, and leveraging fame to build a successful business. By understanding and implementing these strategies, individuals can effectively manage their earnings, create a strong financial foundation, and secure their future.

Section 1: Financial Planning

Financial planning is the process of effectively managing one's finances to achieve personal and financial goals. It involves strategies for budgeting, saving, and investing earnings. Let's explore some key aspects of financial planning:

1.1 Budgeting:
   Budgeting forms the foundation of financial planning. It involves creating a detailed plan for income and expenses, tracking spending habits, and making adjustments to achieve financial goals. For example, a celebrity earning a substantial

income should develop a budget that encompasses various expenses such as housing, transportation, health, entertainment, and philanthropy. By maintaining a budget, they can allocate their earnings wisely and avoid overspending.

## 1.2 Saving:

Saving is crucial for building wealth and establishing financial security. It involves setting aside a portion of earnings for emergencies, future goals, and retirement. Celebrities facing fluctuating income streams should aim to save a certain percentage of their earnings consistently. They can explore various savings options such as high-yield savings accounts, certificates of deposit (CDs), or money market accounts.

## 1.3 Investing:

Investing allows individuals to grow their wealth over time. It involves putting money into various assets such as stocks, bonds, real estate, or mutual funds with the expectation of generating returns. Celebrities can consult financial professionals or hire wealth managers to devise an investment strategy aligned with their financial goals and risk tolerance. Diversification and long-term perspective are crucial for successful investing.

## Section 2: Tax and Legal Considerations

## 2.1 Understanding Tax Obligations:

Fame often brings significant financial rewards, accompanied by increased tax obligations. Celebrities must be aware of various tax categories, including income tax, property tax, sales tax, and estate tax. They should consult tax professionals to ensure compliance, maximize deductions, and develop efficient tax planning strategies. For example, establishing a charitable foundation can not only support causes dear to a celebrity but also provide tax benefits.

2.2 Legal Considerations:

Celebrities face unique legal considerations, such as contracts, endorsements, copyright infringement, and intellectual property rights. They should work closely with lawyers who specialize in entertainment law to protect their interests and navigate legal complexities. Legal professionals can assist in contract negotiation, licensing agreements, and brand protection to secure their financial future.

Section 3: Building a Business

3.1 Leveraging Fame to Create Business Ventures:

Fame provides celebrities with a platform to venture into business opportunities and generate additional income streams. They can leverage their name, influence, and fan base by launching their own products or services. For example, a well-known actor might start a production company, a clothing line, or invest in restaurants or tech startups. These ventures have the potential to generate significant profits beyond their primary source of income.

3.2 Passive Income Streams:

Passive income refers to earnings generated with minimal effort or active involvement. Celebrities can explore passive income opportunities such as investments in real estate, stocks, or royalties from intellectual property. For instance, a musician can earn royalties from songwriting or licensing their music for commercials, movies, or streaming platforms. Passive income streams can provide financial stability and long-term wealth accumulation.

3.3 Scaling Business Ventures:

Once a celebrity establishes a successful business venture, scaling becomes crucial for sustained growth. This involves expanding operations, hiring competent teams, and exploring new markets. Scaling allows celebrities to multiply their earnings and solidify their position as influential entrepreneurs. However, proper financial planning, including budgeting, risk management, and investment strategies, is vital to ensure the growth is sustainable.

Conclusion:

Mastering financial planning, understanding tax and legal obligations, and capitalizing on fame to build successful business ventures are the key pillars of managing finances, building wealth, and ensuring financial security. By implementing these strategies, celebrities can create diversified income streams, mitigate financial risks, and lay a strong foundation for a prosperous future. It is essential to seek professional advice, stay informed about financial trends, and maintain a disciplined approach to achieve long-term financial well-being.

# Chapter 9: Mental and Emotional Well-being: Nurturing a Healthy Mindset

In today's fast-paced world, where demands and expectations are high, it is essential to take care of our mental and emotional well-being. This chapter delves into the importance of developing a healthy mindset and explores strategies for dealing with common challenges such as pressure, stress, success, failure, and seeking support. By adopting coping mechanisms, self-care practices, maintaining a balanced perspective, and building a strong support system, individuals can enhance their mental and emotional well-being.

Section 1: Dealing with Pressure and Stress

Pressure and stress are inevitable aspects of life, but how we handle them can greatly impact our overall well-being. Here, we will explore coping mechanisms and self-care practices that can effectively manage pressure and stress.

Coping Mechanisms:

1. Deep Breathing: Taking slow, deep breaths helps activate

the body's relaxation response, reducing stress and promoting a sense of calm.

Example: When feeling overwhelmed, practicing deep breathing techniques like the 4-7-8 method (inhaling for 4 seconds, holding breath for 7 seconds, and exhaling for 8 seconds) can induce relaxation.

2. Mindfulness Meditation: Engaging in regular mindfulness meditation cultivates awareness of the present moment, reduces stress, and enhances well-being.

Example: Allocating a few minutes each day for meditation, focusing on breathing, and observing thoughts without judgment can promote mental clarity and stress reduction.

3. Physical Exercise: Regular exercise releases endorphins, also known as "feel-good" hormones, reducing stress levels and improving overall mood.

Example: Engaging in activities like running, swimming, or yoga, and aiming for at least 30 minutes of moderate exercise each day can effectively combat stress and pressure.

Self-Care Practices:

1. Prioritizing Rest and Sleep: Getting adequate rest and quality sleep rejuvenates the mind and body, promoting a sense of well-being.

Example: Establishing a consistent bedtime routine, creating a calming sleep environment, and allocating enough time for quality sleep can help manage stress better.

2. Engaging in Hobbies and Activities: Dedicate time to activities that bring joy and relaxation, promoting a sense of fulfillment

and reducing stress.

Example: Pursuing hobbies such as painting, gardening, playing a musical instrument, or reading can provide an outlet for stress relief and relaxation.

3. Practicing Self-Compassion: Being kind to oneself and practicing self-compassion fosters resilience and helps navigate through stressful situations.

Example: Instead of self-criticism, offering yourself understanding, forgiveness, and self-care during challenging times can alleviate stress and promote emotional well-being.

Section 2: Handling Success and Failure

Success and failure are part of life's journey; how we perceive and manage them influences our mental and emotional well-being. This section focuses on maintaining a balanced perspective amidst highs and lows.

Maintaining a Balanced Perspective:

1. Celebrating Achievements with Gratitude: Acknowledging accomplishments with gratitude cultivates a positive mindset and guards against excessive self-criticism.

Example: When achieving a personal or professional goal, taking a moment to reflect on the journey, expressing gratitude towards oneself and others, and celebrating the milestones can foster emotional well-being.

2. Embracing Failure as a Learning Opportunity: Perceiving failure as a stepping stone for growth and learning can help build resilience and prevent negative self-perception.

Example: After experiencing a setback or failure, reflecting on the lessons learned, focusing on personal growth, and setting new goals can foster resilience and instill a sense of purpose.

3. Avoiding Comparison: Comparing oneself to others can lead to feelings of inadequacy, anxiety, and reduced self-esteem. Instead, focus on personal growth and progress.

Example: Rather than comparing achievements or material possessions with others, emphasizing individual strengths, setting realistic goals, and working towards personal improvement can nurture a positive mindset.

Section 3: Seeking Support

Building a strong support system and accessing professional help when needed is crucial for maintaining mental and emotional well-being. This section highlights the significance of seeking support.

Building a Strong Support System:

1. Nurturing Relationships: Cultivating meaningful connections with family, friends, and community strengthens resilience and provides emotional support.

Example: Regularly spending time with loved ones, engaging in open and honest communication, and offering support to others can foster a strong support network.

2. Seeking Peer Support: Connecting with individuals facing similar challenges can provide comfort, understanding, and shared experiences.

Example: Joining support groups, online communities, or participating in group therapy sessions with peers going through similar situations can create a sense of solidarity and support.

Accessing Professional Help:

1. Therapy and Counseling: Seeking professional help from therapists or counselors can provide guidance, coping strategies, and a safe space to explore emotions and experiences.

Example: When facing persistent or overwhelming mental and emotional challenges, reaching out to a licensed therapist or counselor can offer valuable support and guidance.

2. Helplines and Hotlines: Utilizing helplines and hotlines can provide immediate support during times of distress or crisis.

Example: Contacting crisis helplines or hotlines like suicide prevention helplines, domestic violence support lines, or mental health crisis lines can offer immediate assistance during emergencies.

Conclusion:

Building and nurturing a healthy mindset is integral to maintaining mental and emotional well-being. By utilizing coping mechanisms, practicing self-care, maintaining a balanced perspective on success and failure, and seeking support from a strong support system or professionals when needed, individuals can enhance their overall mental and emotional well-being. It is essential to prioritize our mental health, as only then can we truly flourish and lead fulfilling lives.

# Chapter 10: Giving Back to the Community: Making a Difference with Your Fame

In today's society, fame and influence come with great responsibility. Individuals who have achieved fame and success often have a unique opportunity to make a positive impact on their communities and the world at large. This chapter explores three important ways in which individuals can give back to their community and make a meaningful difference: social responsibility, philanthropy and giving, and mentoring and inspiring others. Through these avenues, people can leverage their fame and influence to advocate for causes they believe in, support organizations and initiatives, and empower others to achieve their goals. This chapter delves deeply into each of these topics, providing examples and insights that showcase the profound impact individuals can have when they choose to give back.

Section 1: Social Responsibility
    Using your platform to advocate for causes you believe in

1.1 Definition and Importance of Social Responsibility:

Social responsibility refers to the obligation individuals have to act in ways that promote the well-being and interests of society as a whole. When individuals gain fame and influence, they often have a larger platform to raise awareness and support causes close to their hearts. By using their voice and influence, they can bring attention to social issues and inspire others to take action.

1.2 Examples of Social Responsibility:

a) Environmental Activism: Celebrities like Leonardo Di-Caprio have used their fame to raise awareness about climate change and the importance of environmental conservation. Their efforts have mobilized a global movement and encouraged millions to adopt sustainable practices.

b) Humanitarian Work: Angelina Jolie, through her work with the United Nations High Commissioner for Refugees (UNHCR), has drawn attention to the plight of refugees and displaced people. Her advocacy has led to increased support for humanitarian initiatives and improved conditions for those in need.

Section 2: Philanthropy and Giving

Supporting charitable organizations and initiatives

2.1 Exploring Philanthropy:

Philanthropy involves the donation of time, money, or resources to improve the well-being of others. With fame and success, individuals have the means to make significant contributions to causes they care about. Philanthropy allows them to create long-lasting impacts and address societal issues on a larger scale.

2.2 Examples of Philanthropy:
   a) The Bill & Melinda Gates Foundation: Bill and Melinda Gates, through their foundation, have provided billions of dollars in grants to address global health, education, and poverty. Their efforts have transformed the lives of millions worldwide.

b) Celebrity Foundations: Many famous individuals establish their own foundations to support specific causes. Oprah Winfrey established the Oprah Winfrey Leadership Academy for Girls, providing educational opportunities for underprivileged girls in South Africa.

Section 3: Mentoring and Inspiring Others
   Paying it forward by sharing your knowledge and experiences

3.1 The Power of Mentoring:
   Mentoring involves guiding and inspiring individuals who are seeking personal or professional growth. Sharing knowledge and experiences can empower others to achieve their goals, fostering a positive cycle of success and giving back.

3.2 Examples of Mentoring:
   a) Sports Mentoring: NBA star LeBron James, through his LeBron James Family Foundation, provides mentorship and support to underprivileged children. His initiative aims to help them realize their potentials both on and off the court.

b) Entrepreneurial Mentorship: Business tycoon Richard Branson actively mentors aspiring entrepreneurs, offering advice, resources, and guidance through his various business ventures and platforms. His mentorship has helped numerous individuals achieve business success.

Conclusion:

Giving back to the community is a crucial responsibility for individuals who hold fame and influence. Through social responsibility, philanthropy and giving, and mentoring and inspiring others, individuals can make a profound difference in the lives of those around them. By raising awareness, providing resources, and empowering others, famous individuals have the capacity to create positive change on a global scale. It is through such acts of giving back that individuals truly leave a lasting legacy and inspire others to do the same.

# 50 tips on how to become famous

1. Discover your passion and pursue it wholeheartedly.

2. Develop your skills and talents through practice and dedication.

3. Define your personal brand and portray a unique persona.

4. Network with people in your industry or field.

5. Utilize social media platforms to showcase your work and engage with your audience.

6. Collaborate with other like-minded individuals to expand your reach.

7. Attend industry events and conferences to make connections and gain exposure.

8. Volunteer for local events and charitable organizations to increase your visibility.

9. Build a strong online presence across multiple platforms.

10. Interact with your followers and respond to their comments and messages.

11. Stay up-to-date with current trends and adapt your content accordingly.

12. Create consistent and high-quality content that resonates with your target audience.

13. Use captivating and visually appealing images or videos to capture attention.

14. Engage with popular influencers in your niche to leverage their audience.

15. Be authentic and genuine in your interactions with others.

16. Collaborate with media outlets to get featured or interviewed.

17. Be persistent and don't give up, even in the face of setbacks or rejections.

18. Keep learning and improving your craft to stay ahead of the competition.

19. Seek opportunities for public speaking engagements or guest appearances.

20. Maintain a positive attitude and handle criticism gracefully.

21. Connect with professionals in the entertainment industry for guidance and advice.

22. Utilize search engine optimization techniques to improve your online visibility.

23. Consider hiring a publicist to help manage your public image and media exposure.

24. Engage in philanthropic activities to establish a positive reputation.

25. Create a captivating and memorable personal brand logo or tagline.

26. Seek endorsements from reputable brands or companies in your industry.

27. Leverage the power of viral marketing by creating shareable content.

28. Engage with your local community and build a strong local following.

29. Take part in competitions or talent shows to gain exposure.

30. Attend relevant industry workshops or classes to enhance your skills.

31. Publish content on influential platforms or blogs to raise your profile.

32. Create a website or online portfolio to showcase your work.

33. Be open to new opportunities and collaborations outside your comfort zone.

34. Develop a unique style or persona that sets you apart from others.

35. Consider hiring a talent agent or manager to help with career opportunities.

36. Always be professional and reliable in your interactions with others.

37. Stay updated on the latest industry news and developments.

38. Engage in online debates or discussions related to your field to boost visibility.

39. Attend red carpet events, premieres, or industry parties to network with influential people.

40. Create a strong personal brand narrative that resonates with your audience.

41. Engage with your audience through live streams or Q&A sessions.

42. Develop a signature look or fashion style that becomes your trademark.

43. Utilize crowdfunding platforms to fund your creative projects.

44. Consider creating a YouTube channel or podcast to reach a wider audience.

45. Attend talent competitions or auditions to showcase your skills.

46. Collaborate with local media outlets for interviews or features.

47. Showcase your work at art galleries, exhibitions, or industry showcases.

48. Create compelling and engaging content titles or head-lines.

49. Offer value to your audience through informative or entertaining content.

50. Stay true to yourself and your passion, as authenticity is key to long-term success.

Remember, fame is not an overnight achievement and may come in various forms. Focus on your goals, work hard, and stay dedicated to your craft. Good luck on your journey!